MW01069750

Good luck @ College Oli!

(see pages 74/75)

THANK YOOH!

JM x

4478006R00083

Printed in Germany
by Amazon Distribution
GmbH, Leipzig